Contents

Creamy Potatoes and franks Bake

350 degrees 45 minutes

3 tabs. butter

3 tabs. flour

3 tabs. grated onion

1/2 dry mustard

1 1/2 t, salt

1/4 ts. garlic salt

1 tall can (11 2/3 c.) evaporated milk

1 cup fresh milk

1/4 c. grated Parmesan cheese

2 tabs. chopped parsley

4 c. chopped peeled, cold baked potatoes

6 frankfurters, cut into rings

1. Butter 2 quart. casserole

4. Cook, Stirring constantly, until sauce thickens and boil 1 minute

5. Stir in cheese, parsley, potatoes, and 3/4 franks,

6. Spoon mix into casserole; top with ring of

remaining franks: cover

7. Bake in moderate oven (350 degrees) 45 minutes, or until bubbly.

Baked Beans

1 Large can baked beans

1 lbs Hot dogs cut up

1 Large onion, green pepper add

2 Tsp Molasses

2 T Sugar

1 Tsp Dry Mustard

4 Teaspoons Ketchup

Add to beans and Hot Dogs and

Bake 1 Hour

Chicken Casserole

1 cup broken spaghetti

1 cup Dry bread crumbs

1/4 melted margarine

1 cup grated American cheese

2 Tbs. chopped pimiento

1 or 3 beaten eggs

1 cup diced cooked chicken

1 1/2 cup warm milk

1/2 chopped green pepper

1 teaspoon of salt

Cook spaghetti in boiling salted water,
Drain rinse with hot water
Drain again
Add remaining ingredients
Bake in casserole dish in moderate oven.
Serve mushroom sauce over one 10/2 or
11 ouce can condensed cream of
mushroom soup and a little milk.

Mary's Sausage casserole
1 lb. bulk sausage fry and pour of fat
Mix with: 1 cup celery chopped fine
1/4 cup of green pepper
1 small onion
2 cans whole kernel corn, drained
3 cups cooked rice
and 1 large can tomatoes.
Cook them down separately to shorten
baking time.

Season with with 1/4 teaspoon curry powder, salt, pepper and garlic powder to taste.

Grated Parmesan on top

Bake about 1/2 hour in greased casserole dish.

Scalloped Potatoes Casserole

Cut six potatoes in small pieces.

Make dressing of one pint of milk and 3 tbs flour.

Boil until it thickens add a pinch of butter salt and pepper enough to make it hot.

Put into a pudding dish alternate layers of potatoes and dressing and over the top a layer of brad crumbs. Put small bits of butter over top and bake for 30 minutes

Broccoli Casserole

2 Pks Frozen Broccoli (broken pieces)

1 can Mushroom soup

2/3 Cup evaporated milk 1 1/2 Cups of Parmesan Cheese

Frozen Onion Rings

Mix milk, soup, cheese and pour over broccoli in casserole dish. Bake 350 degrees 25 minutes remove from oven and cover with frozen onion rings. Return to oven bake 10 minutes @ 400 degrees

Beef Casserole

1 lb hamburg

1 onion fried

Put in casserole

2/3 cup drained greed beans

or corn

1 can tomatoes soup

Mix all together top with mashed potatoes
Bake until bubbles over

Clam Casserole

2 Cans minced clams drained

1 can of mushroom soup

1 Cup of milk

1 1/2 Cups Cracker Crumbs

1 Stick of butter

Salt and Pepper
Pour all together and
bake 1 Hour

Green Bean Casserole

1 Lb fresh green beans or canned or frozen

3/4 Milk

1 can Condensed cream of mushroom soup

Add one can of 1/2 cream of chicken

1 can of onions

Combine milk soup, whisk until smooth add beans 1/2 the onions.

Bake in oven @350 degrees

Top with red onions and bake 5 minutes longer

Add a cup of baked chicken season with garlic powder

Chicken Rice Bake

1 Cup washed regular rice

1 Cup Chicken cut up (4 legs-4

thighs-2 2 breast

1 Can mushroom soup

1 Package of Onion soup mix

1 1/2 Cup of water

Wash rice spread in baking dish
Shake chicken with soy mix
put chicken on rice skim side down
sprinkle leftover onion soup mix
over chicken.
Dilute mushroom soup with the
water. Beat with beater.
Add 1 tsp. soy sauce if you wish.
Sprinkle with pepper and paprika.
Bake @ 350 degrees 1 hour.
Turn chicken over add water or milk
if liquid is needed. Bake another 30
minutes until tender.

Zucchini Casserole

4 Cups Zucchini cubed

2 Slices white bread cubed

2 Eggs

2 Teaspoons Onion flakes

2 Oz Grated Parmesan Cheese

1/2 Cup of Skim Milk

Salt and Pepper to taste

Cook Zucchini in slightly salted water until tender

Drain

In large bowl beat eggs and cheese Less 2 Tablespoons move for the top

Slice cube bread, milk, onion flakes, salt and pepper. Add zucchini toss lightly. Place in a loaf pan. Sprinkle top with cheese.

Bake 350 degrees for 35-35 minutes until light and puffy. Serve at once

Lightning Source UK Ltd.
Milton Keynes UK
UKRC010240250321
380816UK00017B/135